LET'S COOK WITH
Cheese!

Delicious & Fun Cheese Dishes Kids Can Make

Nancy Tuminelly

Consulting Editor, Diane Craig, M.A./Reading Specialist

A Division of ABDO
ABDO
Publishing Company

visit us at www.abdopublishing.com

Published by ABDO Publishing Company, a division of ABDO, P.O. Box 398166, Minneapolis, Minnesota 55439. Copyright © 2013 by Abdo Consulting Group, Inc. International copyrights reserved in all countries. No part of this book may be reproduced in any form without written permission from the publisher. Super SandCastle™ is a trademark and logo of ABDO Publishing Company.

Printed in the United States of America, North Mankato, Minnesota
062012
092012

 PRINTED ON RECYCLED PAPER

Editor: Liz Salzmann
Content Developer: Nancy Tuminelly
Cover and Interior Design and Production: Colleen Dolphin, Mighty Media, Inc.
Food Production: Desirée Bussiere
Photo Credits: Colleen Dolphin, Shutterstock, iStockphoto (Gary Milner, Kim Gunkel, Sean Locke, Vanessa Morosini, Dawna Stafford)

The following manufacturers/names appearing in this book are trademarks: Calumet® Baking Powder, Gold Medal® All-Purpose Flour, Lea & Perrins® The Original Worcestershire Sauce, McCormick® Garlic Powder, Old London® Bread Crumbs, Proctor Silex® Hand Blender, Pyrex® Measuring Glass, Roundy's® Cream Cheese, Velveeta® Cheese

Library of Congress Cataloging-in-Publication Data

Tuminelly, Nancy, 1952-
  Let's cook with cheese! : delicious & fun cheese dishes kids can make / Nancy Tuminelly.
    p. cm. -- (Super simple recipes)
  ISBN 978-1-61783-420-2
  1. Cooking (Cheese)--Juvenile literature. I. Title.
  TX759.5.C48T86 2013
  641.6'73--dc23
                          2011052134

Super SandCastle™ books are created by a team of professional educators, reading specialists, and content developers around five essential components—phonemic awareness, phonics, vocabulary, text comprehension, and fluency—to assist young readers as they develop reading skills and strategies and increase their general knowledge. All books are written, reviewed, and leveled for guided reading, early reading intervention, and Accelerated Reader® programs for use in shared, guided, and independent reading and writing activities to support a balanced approach to literacy instruction.

Note to Adult Helpers

Helping kids learn how to cook is fun! It's a great way to practice math and science. Cooking teaches kids about responsibility and boosts their confidence. Plus, they learn how to help out in the kitchen! The recipes in this book require adult assistance. Make sure there is always an adult around when kids are in the kitchen. Expect kids to make a mess, but also expect them to clean up after themselves. Most importantly, make the experience pleasurable by sharing and enjoying the food kids make.

Symbols

Knife
Always ask an adult to help you use knives.

Microwave
Be careful with hot food! Learn more on page 7.

Oven
Have an adult help put things into and take them out of the oven. Learn more on page 7.

Stovetop
Be careful around hot burners! Learn more on page 7.

Nuts
Some people can get very sick if they eat nuts.

Contents

Let's Cook with Cheese!

People love cheese! They have been eating cheese for thousands of years! The first people to make cheese were probably in the Middle East or Central Asia. They taught Europeans how to make cheese. Then Europeans brought cheese to America.

Cheese is made from milk. The milk usually comes from cows, goats, or sheep. Cheese is full of **protein** and **calcium**. Cheese also has a lot of fat. But it is very good for your bones, teeth, and skin.

Cheese comes from all over the world. Some cheese is still made on small farms. Most cheese is made in factories. Cheese comes in many flavors, **textures**, and shapes.

The recipes in this book are simple. It's fun using one main ingredient! Cooking teaches you about food, measuring, and following directions. Enjoy your tasty treats with your family and friends!

Think Safety!

- Ask an adult to help you use knives. Use a cutting board.

- Clean up spills to prevent accidents.

- Keep tools and **utensils** away from the edge of the table or counter.

- Use a step stool if you cannot reach something.

- Tie back long hair or wear a hat.

- Don't wear loose clothes. Roll up long **sleeves**.

- Keep a fire extinguisher in the cooking area.

Cooking Basics

Before you start...

- Get **permission** from an adult.

- Wash your hands.

- Read the recipe at least once.

- Set out all the ingredients and tools you will need.

When you're done...

- Cover food with plastic wrap or aluminum foil. Use **containers** with lids if you have them.

- Wash all of the dishes and **utensils**.

- Put all of the ingredients and tools back where you found them.

- Clean up your work space.

Using the Microwave

- Use microwave-safe dishes.

- Never put aluminum foil or metal in the microwave.

- Start with a short cook time. If it's not enough, cook it some more.

- Use oven mitts when taking things out of the microwave.

- Stop the microwave to stir liquids during heating.

Using the Stovetop

- Turn pot handles away from the burners and the edge of the stove.

- Use the temperature setting in the recipe.

- Use pot holders to handle hot pots and pans.

- Do not leave metal **utensils** in pots.

- Don't put anything except pots and pans on or near the burners.

- Use a timer. Check the food and cook it more if needed.

Using the Oven

- Use the temperature setting in the recipe.

- Preheat the oven while making the recipe.

- Use oven-safe dishes.

- Use pot holders or oven mitts to handle baking sheets and dishes.

- Do not touch oven doors. They can be very hot.

- Set a timer. Check the food and bake it more if needed.

A microwave, stovetop, and oven are very useful for cooking food. But they can be **dangerous** if you are not careful. Always ask an adult for help.

Measuring

Wet Ingredients

Set a measuring cup on the counter. Add the liquid until it reaches the amount you need. Check the measurement from eye level.

Dry Ingredients

Use a spoon to put the dry ingredient in the measuring cup or spoon. Put more than you need in the measuring cup or spoon. Run the back of a dinner knife across the top. This removes the extra.

Moist Ingredients

Moist ingredients are things such as brown sugar and dried fruit. They need to be packed down into the measuring cup. Keep packing until the ingredient reaches the measurement line.

Do You Know This = That?

There are different ways to measure the same amount.

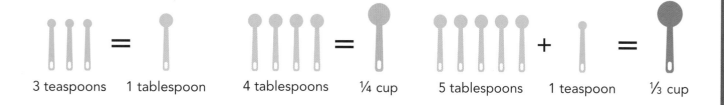

3 teaspoons = 1 tablespoon

4 tablespoons = ¼ cup

5 tablespoons + 1 teaspoon = ⅓ cup

16 tablespoons = 1 cup

1 cup = 8 ounces

1 stick of butter = ½ cup

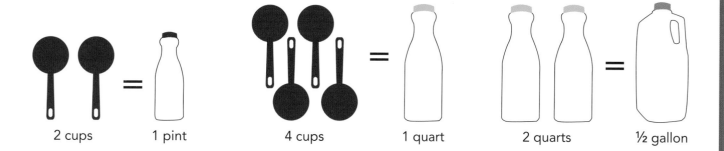

2 cups = 1 pint

4 cups = 1 quart

2 quarts = ½ gallon

Cooking Terms

Mix
Combine ingredients with a mixing spoon. *Stir* is another word for mix.

Melt
Heat something solid until it is softened.

Chop
Cut something into very small pieces with a knife.

Slice
Cut something into thin pieces with a knife.

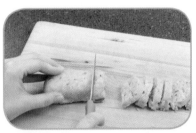

Grate
Shred something into small pieces using a grater.

Coat
Cover something with another ingredient or mixture.

Beat
Stir something with a mixer until it is smooth.

Fry
Cook in hot oil or butter until a brown crust forms.

Cheese, Please!

There are many ways to eat cheese! It is great as a snack with crackers and fruit. You can put it on **sandwiches** and use it in sauces and dips.

American Cheese
Mild. Creamy **texture**.
Great for melting,
sandwiches, snacks.

Cheddar
Mild to sharp. Hard texture.
Great for cooking,
cheese trays, **desserts**,
sandwiches, salads.

Cream Cheese
Very mild. Soft texture.
Great for cooking, desserts,
sandwiches, snacks.

Monterey Jack
Mild. Semi-soft texture.
Great for sandwiches, snacks,
sauces, Mexican dishes.

Mozzarella
Mild. Semi-soft texture.
Great for cooking, pizza,
Italian dishes.

Swiss
Sweet, nutty. Semi-hard texture.
Great for sandwiches, snacks,
salads, desserts.

Tools

sharp knife

9 × 13-inch
baking sheet

mixing spoon

cutting board

grater

paper towels

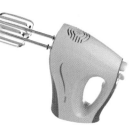

hand mixer

oven mitts

tongs

liquid measuring cup

dry measuring cups

measuring spoons

timer

microwave-safe
bowl

ladle

frying pan

slotted spoon

spatula

fork

pot holders

strainer

plastic wrap

mixing bowls

medium pot

large pot

Ingredients

crispy rice cereal

cinnamon raisin bread

dried basil

paprika

Worcestershire sauce

fresh chives, chopped

apples

potatoes

garlic powder

hot pepper sauce

bread crumbs

carrots

onion

all-purpose flour

vegetable oil

celery

salt & pepper

baking powder

ham, cubed

macaroni noodles

butter

deli ham

rice

pecans

eggs

milk

American cheese

Swiss cheese

cream cheese

Parmesan cheese

Velveeta

cheddar cheese

mozzarella cheese

Colby cheese

Homemade Cheesy Mac

Make your very own macaroni & cheese!

Makes 2 to 4 servings

ingredients

2 cups macaroni noodles

½ cup onion, diced

6 slices American cheese, cut into small pieces

½ cup milk, 2% or whole

pepper

tools

sharp knife

cutting board

measuring cups

large pot

pot holders

strainer

mixing spoon

timer

1. Cook the noodles according to the instructions on the package. Drain the noodles. Put the noodles back in the pot. Add the onions.

2. Add the cheese, milk, and a **dash** of pepper. Stir well.

3. Cook for 4 to 5 minutes over medium heat. Stir often.

4. Remove the pot from the heat. Let it sit for 3 minutes.

TIP: Don't use skim milk. The sauce will be too watery.

Creamy Cheese Dip

This is a perfect snack for parties or sleepovers!

Makes 4 servings

ingredients

2 tablespoons butter

2 tablespoons all-purpose flour

7 slices American cheese, torn into small pieces

½ teaspoon salt

1 cup milk, 2% or whole

tools

microwave-safe bowl

measuring spoons

oven mitts

mixing spoon

measuring cups

1. Put the butter in a microwave-safe bowl. Cook it in the microwave on high for 15 seconds. Mix in the flour. Mix in the cheese and salt.

2. Add the milk. Stir well. Cook in the microwave on high for 2 minutes.

3. Stir to remove lumps. Cook it in the microwave for 2 more minutes.

4. Repeat step 3 until the cheese is completely melted. The dip will be smooth. Serve warm with chips or veggies!

TIP: Don't use skim milk. The dip will be too watery.

Italian Cheese Bites

Delicious rice and cheese appetizers!

Makes 10 balls

ingredients

2 cups rice, cooked
2 eggs, beaten
½ teaspoon salt
¼ teaspoon pepper
½ teaspoon dried basil
⅓ cup Parmesan cheese, grated
½ cup mozzarella cheese, cubed
½ cup bread crumbs
vegetable oil

tools

whisk
grater
mixing bowls
mixing spoon
measuring cups
measuring spoons
sharp knife

cutting board
large frying pan
slotted spoon
paper towels
pot holders
timer

1 Mix the rice and eggs in a bowl. Mix in the salt, pepper, basil, and Parmesan cheese. Chill for 1 hour.

2 Roll the rice mixture into balls. Make them about the size of golf balls. Put a cube of mozzarella cheese in the middle of each ball.

3 Roll the balls in the bread crumbs, Make sure the balls are completely coated.

4 Put about ½ inch (1 cm) of oil in the frying pan. Heat the oil for 1 minute over medium-high heat. Put the rice balls in the pan. Fry for 1 to 2 minutes or until golden. Use a slotted spoon to take the balls out of the pan.

5 Put the balls on a paper towel. Cool for 5 minutes.

Nutty Cheese Nibbler

A scrumptious spread everyone will love!

Makes 1 cheese ball

ingredients

16 ounces Colby cheese

8 ounces Velveeta

3 ounces cream cheese, softened

1 teaspoon Worcestershire sauce

garlic powder

1 teaspoon paprika

¾ cup pecans, finely chopped

tools

grater

large bowl

hand mixer

measuring spoons

cutting board

sharp knife

measuring cups

1 Grate the Colby and Velveeta cheeses. Put them in a large bowl.

2 Add the cream cheese. Beat with the mixer on medium. Beat until the mixture is smooth.

3 Add the Worcestershire sauce and a **dash** of garlic powder. Mix well. Form the cheese mixture into a ball.

4 Sprinkle paprika on the cutting board. Roll the ball over the paprika until it is coated.

5 Spread the pecans on the cutting board. Roll the ball over the pecans until it is coated. Serve with bread or crackers!

Great Grilled Cheese

The best cheese sandwich with lots of goodies!

Makes 2 sandwiches

ingredients

4 slices cinnamon raisin bread
2 slices cheddar cheese
2 slices Swiss cheese
1 apple, peeled, cored,
    and sliced
2 slices deli ham
2 tablespoons butter
¼ cup milk
2 eggs

tools

cutting board
sharp knife
frying pan
measuring cups
fork
medium mixing bowl
spatula
timer

1. Lay 2 slices of bread on the cutting board. On each slice, put 1 slice of cheddar cheese, 1 slice of Swiss cheese, half the apple slices, and 1 slice of ham. Place the other slices of bread on top to make **sandwiches**. Press down gently.

2. Melt the butter in the frying pan over medium heat.

3. Put the milk and eggs in a bowl. Mix them well with a fork.

4. Dip each sandwich in the egg mixture. Turn them over until they are coated.

5. Put the sandwiches in the frying pan. Fry on each side for 2 minutes. The bread should be golden brown and the cheese should be melted.

Fried Cheese Fritters

These savory biscuits go great with any dinner!

Makes 6 servings

ingredients

⅔ cup vegetable oil

1¼ cup all-purpose flour

1 teaspoon salt

2 teaspoons baking powder

1 egg

⅔ cup milk

¾ cup cheddar cheese, grated

tools

grater

frying pan

measuring cups

measuring spoons

mixing bowls

mixing spoon

fork

hand mixer

pot holders

tongs

paper towels

1 Mix the flour, salt, and baking powder together in a large bowl.

2 Put the egg and milk in a medium bowl. Mix them well with a fork.

3 Slowly pour the wet mixture into the dry mixture. Beat with the mixer on medium.

4 Use a mixing spoon to gently fold in the cheese.

5 Heat the oil in the frying pan over medium-high heat. Put heaping tablespoons of the mixture in the frying pan. Fry them until they are browned.

6 Use tongs to take the fritters out of the pan. Place them on a paper towel.

3

4

5

Cheeselicious Chowder

A hearty and nutritious cheesy soup

Makes 4 servings

ingredients

2 cups potatoes, diced
½ cup carrots, sliced
½ cup celery, sliced
¼ cup onion, chopped
1½ teaspoon salt
¼ teaspoon pepper
¼ cup butter
¼ cup all-purpose flour
2 cups milk
2 cups cheddar cheese, grated
1 cup ham, cubed

tools

grater
pot holders
measuring cups & spoons
sharp knife
cutting board
medium pot

timer
mixing spoon
large pot
ladle
serving bowls

1 Boil 2 cups of water in a medium pot. Add the potatoes, carrots, celery, onion, salt, and pepper. Put the lid on the pot. Cook over low heat for 10 minutes. Remove from heat.

2 Mix the butter, flour, and milk in a large pot. Cook over medium heat.

3 Add the cheese. Stir until it is melted. Mix in the ham.

4 Pour the vegetable mixture into the cheese mixture. Cook on low heat until it steams. Do not let it boil.

5 Use a ladle to put the soup in serving bowls.

TIP: If you want thicker soup, use more flour and cheese.

Cheddar Crispies

A cheesy snack with a crunch!

Makes 54 snacks

ingredients

1 cup butter, softened

3 cups cheddar cheese, grated

2 cups all-purpose flour

¼ cup fresh chives, chopped

½ teaspoon salt

½ teaspoon hot pepper sauce

¼ teaspoon garlic powder

2 cups crispy rice cereal

tools

grater	cutting board
measuring cups	plastic wrap
large mixing bowl	9 × 13-inch baking sheet
mixing spoon	timer
measuring spoons	oven mitts
sharp knife	ruler

1. Mix the butter and cheese in a large bowl. Mix in the flour, chives, salt, hot pepper sauce, and garlic powder. Add the rice cereal. Mix well.

2. Divide the mixture into four pieces. Roll them into 6-inch (15 cm) logs.

3. Wrap the logs in plastic wrap. Chill them for 1 hour.

4. Preheat the oven to 325 **degrees**. Cut the logs into ¼-inch (1 cm) slices. Put them on the baking sheet.

5. Bake for 20 to 25 minutes, until the edges are lightly brown. Let them cool.

Glossary

calcium – a natural element that is needed for good health, especially for healthy teeth and bones.

container – something that other things can be put into.

dangerous – able or likely to cause harm or injury.

dash – a very small amount added with a quick, downward shake.

degree – the unit used to measure temperature.

dessert – a sweet food, such as fruit, ice cream, or pastry, served after a meal.

permission – when a person in charge says it's okay to do something.

protein – a substance needed for good health, found naturally in meat, eggs, beans, nuts, and milk.

sandwich – two pieces of bread with a filling, such as meat, cheese, or peanut butter, between them.

sleeve – the part of a piece of clothing that covers some or all of the arm.

texture – what something feels like, such as rough, smooth, hard, or soft.

utensil – a tool used to prepare or eat food.